ACTS OF CRUCIFIXION

KECHI NOMU

This is a work of fiction. All names, characters, places, and incidents are a product of the author's imagination. Any resemblance to real events or persons, living or dead, is entirely coincidental.

Published by Akashic Books

ISBN: 978-1-61775-631-3

Printed in China through Four Colour Print Group, Louisville, Kentucky
First printing

Akashic Books
Brooklyn, New York, USA
Ballydehob, Co. Cork, Ireland
Twitter: @AkashicBooks
Facebook: AkashicBooks
E-mail: info@akashicbooks.com
Website: www.akashicbooks.com

African Poetry Book Fund
Prairie Schooner
University of Nebraska
110 Andrews Hall
Lincoln, Nebraska 68588

TABLE OF CONTENTS

PREFACE
by Safia Elhillo

In *Acts of Crucifixion*, Nigerian poet Kechi Nomu's poems feel simultaneously futuristic, immediate, and ancient. What is initially striking about this work is the feeling of synchronicity, of interconnectivity, that the poet skillfully constructs with her fluid handling of time and character. Especially striking (in a moment where the semi- or fully autobiographical *I* is the sole concern of many poems and collections of poems) are all the people in Nomu's poems— poems populated with lovers, fathers, mothers, boys, Eves, and ghosts—speaking and spoken about in cacophony to give this work a feeling of congregation. As a result, remarkably, these poems—though not without their aches—do not succumb to the primary risk of deep self-reflection: loneliness. Their characters are given exquisite attention in the hands of the speaker, who writes with equal care about we, they, she, he, you, and the occasional, beautifully timed clarity of the *I*.

Nomu builds, in this chapbook, a Möbius strip of a world that begins over and over, where events of the past continue to happen, where forgetting is impossible. In the poem "Waterwalls," we are placed in several time periods concurrently—maybe Frida Kahlo is still alive while a pharaoh drowns biblically in the Red Sea, and

> a woman waits at the border
> to cross a red (already) sea
> without her staff & papers.

In a moment that could be B.C. or A.D. or yesterday or still happening.

In "3 Women," the speaker's maternal grandmother dies, "Every day . . . in her lover's arms," rising again each day to die once more, in an endless loop. This transcendence of linear time, in a poem which establishes its concern with lineage across three generations, positions the speaker's lineage as horizontal,

rather than vertical—those who came before are never left behind and continue
to exist alongside the speaker. They are still coiling through time, their stories
forming concentric circles around those of their descendants.

These poems create a world in which time and location melt together in a
metaphysical sort of synesthesia. Time becomes a place to leave and return to;
a place opening and closing with the growth of the trees; a place that one can
outgrow; and a place that "do[es] not hold us"—as beautifully rendered in "A
Poem about Falling"—"The world begins again where a rubber tree has grown
to touch the roof," where the poem's protagonists "fall out of that year like fruits
too ripe, / from trees that do not hold us."

Just as time shifts and transforms in these poems, bodies shape-shift to become
landscapes, to become the world itself, as the body of the boy in "Note to the Boy
Kicking the Stone" blurs in and out of its own shape, into a larger topography:

> The boy's body
> bends
> to pick the stone
>
> and you see how
> his body too is a road
> with curves,
> too many
>
> Curves.
>
> Once or twice
> you
> see
> the bones
> of his
> vertebrae

become

hills.

In "Postscript: Four Boys are Murdered One Morning in Aluu," the protagonists "try to hold palms over [their] faces but the world rushes in," and this open border between the world and the self is central to the concerns of this collection—everything is personal, everything is political, everything is intimate and large. These poems' fluid relationship between the world and the self and their striking psychogeography position Kechi Nomu as a literary descendant of Senegal's Léopold Sédar Senghor, who wrote in his *For Kora:* "My desire is to learn your land better to learn you."

Nomu's deft weaving of landscapes and characters creates an omnipresent sense of oneness between the elements of this work. This is illustrated most compellingly in the blurring between the earthly and the divine—one finds, in these poems, "a concrete / Eden" ("A Poem About Falling"), "seconds as Eden . . . as hell" ("My Father Sings"), "sunlight arrang[ing] itself in the shape of a cross" ("Sometimes a Man Tries to Hang Himself on a Wooden Cross"), with biblical imagery as a central motif throughout the collection, once more, making the ancient (the Bible itself) and the future (the promise of Eden) a part of the contemporary landscape. Men still hang from crosses, palms bleeding, this time by their own knives. Other bodies hang from trees, calling back to another past that blurs into the present: "shoes hanging on nails to the wall / in sensible acts of crucifixion" ("Acts of Crucifixion"). Eden is on Earth, in the concrete, in the seconds where children anticipate the return of their fathers. And hell is too, in the same seconds.

This collection showcases, stunningly, Kechi Nomu's aptitude for cacophony, her ability to build and populate a brilliant, bustling world. Nomu is a tender, vivid storyteller, with a gift for imbuing a compelling voice and psyche to each character she writes, however brief the rendering. Hers is a voice, to use her own words from "Postscript: Four Boys are Murdered One Morning in Aluu": "Exactly the shape of throats, exactly memory."

This collection is alive with the stories she carries, which she immortalizes with these poems.

NOTE TO THE BOY KICKING THE STONE

The boy's body
bends
to pick the stone

and you see how
his body too is a road
with curves,
too many

Curves.

Once or twice
you
see
the bones
of his
vertebrae
become
hills.

Here, a story begins,
rises, falls,
and ends
in
ghosts.

A POEM ABOUT FALLING

That year we climb the backstairs nobody uses, careful
to sidestep the places where cracks are visible.
It does not cave and we do not fall.
Up, in a concrete

Eden, we lay on the old mattress we find.
Warmed by years of sun, our bodies touch & entwine.
The world begins again where a rubber tree has grown to touch the roof,
where it opens to let the sun touch skin;
you and I, Eves.

When we fall, we fall out of that year like fruits too ripe,
from trees that do not hold us.
Me, into a penance where the heart is never enough
and the world only lets me touch it
bone to cervix. You into men
whose faces begin to swallow your own.

YOUR OLD BONES ARE SEEKING WOODEN CROSSES

Your father is a sinner.
You have seen the fire
in his eyes before it burns
people in their dreams. Sometimes on these streets,
when your heart becomes too big to hold in one place, you walk
as if everything is a debt
payable in sweat.

Here, on a jetty in Boyo,
you sit, let your legs dangle over the edge

like the other boys
waiting for their fathers.
You want to walk on water so bad
or to tell your father you know
what it is to sin,
but you let him pile dreams broken on you
instead. They become the stones
you cast
on water—confessions—
watch them sink.

Your old bones are seeking
wooden crosses.

SOMETIMES A MAN TRIES TO HANG HIMSELF
ON A WOODEN CROSS

(After Hissène Habré, A Chadian Tragedy)

But sometimes a man tries with his hands
to trace the shape of the rope they tried to hang him with,
or the size of his prison.

This big. This wide. This empty. He stands where the things left behind are standing,
or crumbling or begging to be loved,

lets his body touch the earth where
sunlight arranges itself in the shape of a cross.
He only wants to exhume his heart if he can find it here
in front of a blue door.

On all the other days he drives a bike beyond sunset
down, down into the village where he was born.
Here, they say memories of the old wars will heal him,
a little of the love still burning,
a little of the places inside him where his bones have been bent,
broken.

MY FATHER SINGS

This is what the road forgives
in hell: the faces of our children carved in stone
and the voices of people speaking our names from their dreams,
soft: *come, come, touch me here.*

In daylight we do not remember things hidden beneath the bodies
of women we held in places we cannot remember,
and how we said their names, the names of their children,
their memories making islands outside your heart.

In your cities at night, your children die waiting for you to walk through doors
not there. You are finding doors in bodies. These seconds as Eden, as the fall of
man, as hell
when you touch their faces again, palms shaking heavy with the scent of stamen
and shots inside you. Just so that you can walk over bridges.

You, the man disappearing into dew in the morning,
the world behind you becoming water.

I will tell you this,
once I saw a man like me take a knife to the center of his hands to crucify himself, to show us where, how he bleeds.

A PORTRAIT OF MY MOTHER'S LOVER
AS AN ANONYMOUS MAN

Sometimes, you reduce him to this:
the place at the back of his head where all the hairs have begun to fall out.
Still, he becomes the size of memory
swelling in your chest. Inside, he sits on that chair in front of a house
you are afraid of. These walls where his pictures hang, soft with a bricklayer's
hand and his secret women, have become like the old boulders by the River
Ethiope: alive with pain, watermarks. A crack on the wall for each year,
everything his eyes have touched.

3 WOMEN

These memories are my mother's
of her mother,
a woman, faceless, body floating in sand & air.
Every day she dies in her lover's arms,
she who sang the praise songs of dead men,
a voice carrying the swell of the years,
offering rice, milk, water to wandering men
who came to her to drink the dark red wine of sin.
I want to say her name long enough to shake her bones,
if only I knew where to find them.
I want to die in my lover's arms,
a woman, faceless,
body floating in sand & air.

My mother,
afraid to say her mother's name,
makes it the shape of prayers,
feeds us God, telling us God will love us more
if we are women without hungers,
our faces unadorned,
no eyeliners for seduction,
no red for our lips,
our bodies holy,
virgins waiting for the rapture of men.

This memory is mine:
of a girl, name unknown.

She dies carrying a bomb,

head severed from her body,
memories severed.
Body floating in sand & air.
She only wanted to see God.

Afraid to say her name,
I make it the shape of a prayer.

IT COMES IN WAVES

(for Ugo)

Backyard
Home, the rubbish heap flourishing
more rubbish, lush grass
compost monument.
Here, we used to dream of swimming in
chlorine-blue water, sipping sangrias,
the dreams forever outside of ourselves
made of fragments of other countries happy on television.

1996
For three weeks you love him,
your bodies hanging like fruits too ripe from the wrong trees,
and then you never see him again.

12:30 a.m., 26th of April, 2014
Google search history: has Jonathan Cheban found love?
And then you type in the search words for him, for longing. You do not get
a *404 Bad Request—Check your spelling for the requested URL*.
You do not find him.

You fall asleep to this & the walls of your bedroom throbbing with the prayers
of a church on your street.

Upon discovering what an autobahn is
If the world breaks here, where will the cracks begin?
How long before it reaches us if walls are made of flesh?

It comes in waves

You are lying face up on a river.
Floating. You have never been on water like this.
Underneath, the world is sand and the nibble of small fish.
If you died this way,
crashing against the abutment of a bridge in Ofufe Nza,
who will see how your memories have lived on your body?
Who will know that this was not a happy memory?

ACTS OF CRUCIFIXION

This is where all the poetry begins;
on a street
where a body has bombed itself in search of God.
Like everybody else who sees this,
you make a passing inventory:
unmarked places,
unclaimed body parts.
You say you are not afraid of what love has done to you

until names whispered in the streets start to grow inside your skin.
Name after name, city after city. Inside you, houses implode,
bend, like rods failing in concrete,
until what is left unmarked is an unlikely memory:
your mother's shoes hanging on nails to the wall
in sensible acts of crucifixion.

Besides their worn heels, no stories are left behind for her children.

GIVING HEAD

Overnight the world becomes full
of smiling people
and I take you by hand
to a room because it means nothing
and because at some point you will hear me
say this in a dream where I am talking to myself:

*I have been sore for years. I have been trying to repeat a nineties love song for mood.
I have been conjuring a decade with its sea of hearts. There are places we have loved
where the houses keep coming down. I have grown accustomed to the children playing
with the ghosts of things in the ruins.*

In this dream, I kneel
because I have to find ways
to hide the skin on my face
from recognition.
Mouthful, how long does a person not breathe
before they stop altogether?

TO GIVE YOUR HEART TO A BROKEN CITY

On a bus, it is easy to make out the ways that a city is broken.
A street, empty, wants to wear itself heavy on the heart.
Here and there on roads we never return to
our eyes hold the different ways
a body bears weights.
We see how people come and go
without becoming people who break.
Inside, radio songs fill us with the different forms of loneliness.
Later, home, you sit with me like this
in a routine where we let muted lights from an LCD
come and go, its own cycles in our eyes—
these incalculable equations of loss.
Nothing here bears the exact weight of love.
We do not stop to tell ourselves how we used to be so in love
with a country. Memory rejects the scene
where a house once stood.

WATERWALLS

It begins with Kahlo in a picture.
Here, she is letting her eyebrows grow
into themselves. And here too, a boy
does not see how he breaks your heart.
He citizen, you foreigner, standing only inches from him.

Like the necessity of shadows overlapping,
he says into Kahlo's face,
the lighting here is good for pictures,
so that inside you feel what it is:
your ship sinking . . . sea caving under the weight of dreams,
and these waterwalls in a chest of flesh.

Some days, they rise so high
it is impossible not to feel what you are or
see, again, how a Pharaoh drowns running away
from his waterwalls towards you,
without chariots, how a woman waits at the border
to cross a red (already) sea
without her staff & papers.

You see this, standing
so close to the length of your own shadow,
so close you know what it feels like:

All the caves of a body's silence . . .

A LABYRINTH IS BORN ON YOUR SKIN

CMS

This is how you lose your way home,
eyes loving the stained glass of a church window,
your head, filament in light bulb, becoming fantasy.

This is how a labyrinth is born on your skin:

the prophecies and prose of your country
opening pores first: sweat,
then blood, then love.

And love: doing a caesarean thing in your chest.
Inside you: beast trapped in car light at dusk,
giving birth to another beast.
Inside you: still loving countries by their names
and Gods by their beauty.

NIGHT MARKET

Yaba

Again we cross the rail tracks into the dark of night market.
Here, men gather around a small fire to remember the day.

We watch the women feed the fire.
                              We watch the fire swallow the faces of men.

Not far from here, on the bridge where the world
fell from a MAERSK shipping truck on
the bodies of people coming and going,
containing all our hearts,

our dead did not become angels or gods.

POSTSCRIPT: FOUR BOYS ARE MURDERED
ONE MORNING IN ALUU

Four boys die young. Cause of death—Jungle Justice.
Their bodies, the throbbing parts of the earth, do not become sinkholes.

But I am telling you there is a fierceness to these things:
A body letting itself be penetrated by all these forms of love at once.

Women in a church beyond the fence begin their early morning solemn singing.
Their voices fitting like fists, exactly the shape of throats, exactly memory.

I am telling you there is a fierceness to these things:
A body letting itself be penetrated by all these forms of love at once.

Dawn becoming darkness. Rain hitting an old drum where the water has
gathered for years, no different from dead souls receiving love. Forlorn in a
room where the darkness is never enough to hide you.

I am telling you there is a fierceness to these things:
A body letting itself be penetrated by all these forms of love at once.

The shadows, never enough to fill the spaces between us. So, in the beginning,
we try to hold palms over our faces but the world rushes in.

I am telling you there is a fierceness to these things:
A body letting itself be penetrated by all these forms of love at once.

He, touching my flesh. Rubbing the dark rumpled surface over my nipples.
Inside, I feel the empty beneath flesh.

A body letting itself be penetrated by all these forms of love at once.

And streets in aftermath do not become ballads
in our throats.

MEMORY

Me,
holding the edge of the world before we fall into water.
Tonight,
a street stands in its sepia silence.

Your memory,
jellyfish soft,
unguent hungry,
eats everything in plain sight
because the past wants to speak to you.

ACKNOWLEDGMENTS

"Giving Head" first appeared in Expound
"Waterwalls" first appeared in *Tuesday Poem* (Dami Ajayi's blog)
"A Portrait of My Mother's Lover as an Anonymous Man" first
appeared in the *Bangalore Review*